# The Voice
## and Singing

### Rita Storey

A+

**Smart Apple Media**

Smart Apple Media
P.O. Box 3263, Mankato, Minnesota 56002

Printed in the United States of America at Corporate Graphics in North Mankato, Minnesota

Published by arrangement with the Watts Publishing Group Ltd, London.

Art director: Jonathan Hair
Series designed and created by Painted Fish Ltd.
Designer: Rita Storey
Editor: Fiona Corbridge
Adviser: Helen MacGregor

Picture credits
© Barrie Harwood LRPS LBPPA/ Alamy p. 12, Geoff A. Howard/ Alamy p. 16; CBSO/Adrian Burrows pp. 13, 17, 18 and 19; © Gero Breloer/ dpa/ Corbis p. 25, © Rune Hellestad/ Corbis p. 15, © Anders Ryman/ Corbis p. 14; istockphoto.com pp. 6, 7, 13, 18, 19, 20, 21 and 22; Tas Kyprianou/ Scottish Opera p. 24; Tudor Photography pp. 3, 4, 5, 8, 9, 10, 11, 23 and 26; Ulster Orchestra p. 24.

Cover images: Geoff A. Howard/ Alamy (bottom middle); Tudor Photography, Banbury (top); istock.com (bottom left and bottom right)

All photos posed by models.
Thanks to Hannah Barton, Indya Clayton, Maddi Indun, and George Stapleton.

Library of Congress Cataloging-in-Publication Data

Storey, Rita.
  The voice and singing / Rita Storey.
    p. cm. -- (Let's make music)
  Includes index.
  Summary: "Gives examples of different types of singing, along with introductions on different ways of performing together and reading music"-- Provided by publisher.
  ISBN 978-1-59920-216-7 (hardcover)
  1. Singing--Juvenile literature.  I. Title.
  MT898.S76 2010
  782--dc22

                                2008040698

022310
1204

# Contents

Words in **bold** are in the glossary.

# The Voice

**Everyone owns a special musical instrument—their voice. We can use our voice to sing.**

Your voice can make different sounds when you sing or speak. You can make it very quiet if you want to whisper, or you can shout or scream and make it louder.

If you are cheering your favorite team, your voice will be very loud.

## Different Voices

We can recognize people we know just by hearing their voice. Each voice has its own **tone** or **timbre**.

## Happy or Sad?

We use our voice to express how we feel. You can tell if someone is happy or sad just by the sound of his or her voice.

When you answer the phone, you recognize friends by their voice.

# Making a Sound

**When you breathe in and out normally, it does not make any sound.**

## Breathing In
When you breathe in, air goes into your lungs.

## Breathing Out
When you breathe out, a muscle called the diaphragm (a bit like a trampoline stretched across the inside of your body) moves upwards to push the air out of your lungs.

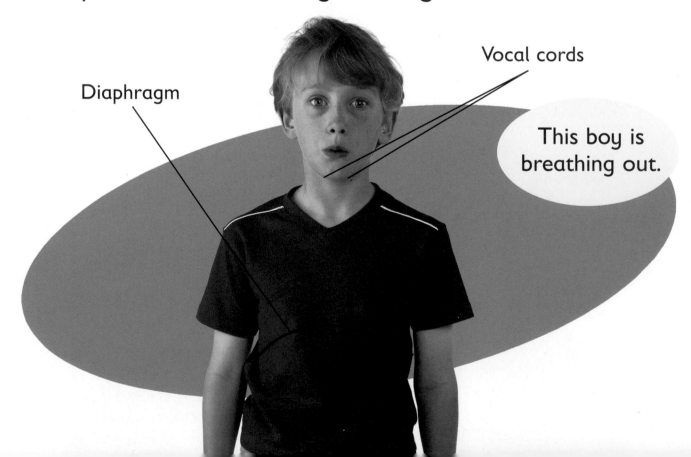

Diaphragm

Vocal cords

This boy is breathing out.

8

The air that you breathe out goes through the opening in your throat.

## Vibrations

There are muscles called vocal cords around the opening of your throat. When you speak or sing, the air you breathe out is forced past the vocal cords and makes them **vibrate**.

## Sound Waves

The vibrations make **sound waves** that travel through the air. Sound waves make the sounds you can hear.

### Music Notes

If you make a sound with your lips closed, it is called humming.

This girl's vocal cords are vibrating.

# Singing

**When you make musical sounds with your voice, it is called singing.**

## Mouth Shape

The shape you make with your mouth when you sing changes the sound of your voice. Try making a small, round "o" shape with your lips, then sing a long "ooo" sound on one note.

These children are singing "Happy Birthday."

These mouth shapes help make very different sounds.

## Different Sounds

Now, as you sing "ooo," gradually change your lips into a smile. Can you hear the sound changing?

Try singing other vowel sounds— "aaa," "eee," "oh," "ow"—and notice all the different mouth shapes and sounds you make.

# Different Singers

Katherine Jenkins is a singer from the United Kingdom.

**Some singing voices are high and some are low. We say they have a high pitch or a low pitch.**

Men's voices have a deeper pitch than women's because their vocal cords are bigger. There are special names for different singing voices.

The four most common kinds of singing voice are:

Soprano—high female voice.
Alto—low female voice.
Tenor—high male voice.
Bass—low male voice.

**Listen!**
Page 28 tells you about various singers you can listen to.

## Treble

Boys have a high singing voice, which is called a treble. As a boy grows, his vocal cords get longer. When he is a teenager, his voice goes from high pitch to a lower pitch (we say it "cracks").

A man's voice is deep; a boy's voice is high.

# Why Do We Sing?

**Singing is a way of expressing how we feel.**

## Celebration

Singing is something we do when we are happy. People sing to celebrate special events like weddings. We sing our national anthem at sporting events.

In some countries, people welcome guests with a song.

## Protest Singers

Some singers write songs about what they think is wrong in the world. These songs are called protest songs. Sometimes people will listen more to the words of a song than if you just spoke plainly about the issue.

## Stories

People sing songs that tell stories about things that have happened. These songs help people remember the past.

Bob Dylan is famous for his protest songs.

# Choirs

**People often get together to sing. A group of singers who practice and sing together is called a choir.**

Singing is an important part of some religions. Some churches have a choir that sings to music played on an organ. Some choirs include young boys who sing treble (high)— they are called choirboys.

These girls are part of a youth chorus.

## Different Choirs

There are many different types of choirs. A male voice choir is a large choir of men. There are also women's choirs and mixed choirs. A youth choir, or **chorus**, is one that is just for young people. The different kinds of voices in a choir give it its own special sound.

# Sing to the Music

This picture shows a symphony chorus and a children's chorus on stage together.

**Some choirs are very big. They may sing with an orchestra.**

A large choir with many singers, which performs in big **concert** halls with a **symphony** orchestra, is called a chorus or symphony chorus.

## Music Notes

Music that is specially written so that it can be sung by a choir or chorus is called an arrangement. Different voices sing different parts of the arrangement.

## Smaller Choirs

A chamber choir is much smaller than a symphony chorus. Chamber choirs sometimes perform without musical **accompaniment**.

Singing without a musical accompaniment is called singing "a cappella."

## Barbershop Quartets

A barbershop quartet is four people with singing voices that blend together in close harmony. They sing a cappella.

# Sing Along

**You don't have to join a choir to sing with other people.**

## Choose a Style

There are many different styles of singing. Soul, jazz, folk, blues, rock, country, and pop are just a few of them.

This is a rock band in concert.

A soul singer

You can use your voice in different ways to express emotions. Some singers sound very sad, but others can make you feel happy.

## Singing in a Band

Bands and groups may have a lead singer who sings the main part of the song, and backup singers who provide harmonies in the background.

# Songs

This girl is being taught a song by her voice instructor.

**Words that have been set to music are called songs.**

### Parts of a Song

The words in a song are known as **lyrics**. The lyrics are often broken into a number of **verses** and a chorus that is repeated after each verse.

## Music Notes

The words of a song are sung to a **melody** or tune. The melody, or tune, of a piece of music makes it different from any other piece of music. This is the important part!

The speed at which a song is sung is called its **tempo**.

22

## Learning a Song

We learn songs by listening to other people sing them. We copy what they do.

A singer has to learn to sing the correct musical notes at the right pitch. This is called singing in tune.

Each note has to be sung for the right length of time.

## Music Notes

The music and lyrics of a song can also be written down so that people can learn them.

Music is written in musical notes. There are **symbols** to tell us how long or short a note is, or how high or low it is.

A long note    A short note    A low note    A high note

The musical notes of a song are shown with the words underneath. This is called a music score.

23

# Performing

People like to go and listen to singers performing on stage.

## Opera

An opera is a **play** in which the story is sung, not spoken. Operas can be serious or funny. Many countries have their own national opera company.

### Music Notes

**Fit to perform**
Professional singers do voice exercises to increase the **range** of notes that they can sing, and to avoid hurting their vocal cords. They will also do **warm-up exercises** before a performance.

A scene from an opera called *Madam Butterfly*.

Singers from the musical *Mamma Mia*.

## Musical Theater

Musicals are plays that use music, songs, speech, and dance to tell a story. The performances can be very energetic.

## Concerts

When singers or musicians perform on stage in front of an audience, it is called a concert. Concerts are given in theaters, concert halls, or even sports stadiums.

# Let's All Sing!

**When do you sing? Do you sing at football games or in the shower? Do you sing to your favorite songs on the radio? Maybe you sing karaoke?**

Whether you are singing alone or with other people, singing can make you feel happy. So why not sing more often? Get some friends together and sing your favorite songs.

Singing karaoke can be fun.

# Listen!

## Web Sites

Look for the lyrics of well-known children's songs in the Musical Mouseum (hosted by a mouse) at:
*www.kididdles.com/lyrics/index.html*

Find your favorite songs, including songs from movie soundtracks, on this karaoke site and then sing along at:
*www.niehs.nih.gov/kids/music.htm*

Visit *Mary Poppins*, the musical. Click on "Fun Stuff" to watch videos or listen to songs such as "Supercalifragilistic..." at:
*www.marypoppinsthemusical.com*

Find out about singers who sing with the New York Philharmonic Orchestra. Take a walk backstage to find the dressing rooms and read about Barbara Bonney (soprano), Ian Bostridge (tenor) and the boys' choir of Harlem at:
*www.nyphilkids.org/dressingrooms/*

Look at diagrams of how the voice works inside the human body and watch a slow-motion film of the vocal cords at:
*http://thesingingvoice.com/index.html*

Listen to the amazing sounds that the famous vocalist Bobby McFerrin can make with his voice. You can hear him performing a cappella music at:
*www.bobbymcferrin.com*

Watch a video clip from the Indianapolis Children's Choir about why they love singing together at:
*www.icchoir.org*

# CDs

### Songs
Various artists: *Disney's Greatest, Volume One.*
Elizabeth Mitchel: *You Are My Flower.*

### Soloists
Katherine Jenkins: *Première.*
Aled Jones: *You Raise Me Up* (includes "Walking in the Air").
Bobby McFerrin: *Mouth Music; Medicine Music; Beyond Words.*

### Choirs
Various choirs: *Hallelujah! Great Sacred Choruses.*
Ladysmith Black Mambazo: *Raise Your Spirit Higher.*

### Opera
Humperdinck: *Hansel and Gretel.*
Mozart: *The Magic Flute.*
Britten: *Noye's Fludde.*

### Musicals
Andersenn/Ulvaeus: *Mamma Mia.*
Bernstein: *West Side Story.*
Elton John: *The Lion King* (soundtrack).

### Barbershop
The Dapper Dans: *Shave and a Haircut.*

# Glossary

**Accompaniment**  The playing of an instrument to support a singer or musician as he or she performs.

**Chorus**  This has two meanings: a type of choir, or part of a song that is repeated after each verse.

**Concert**  A performance by musicians or singers on stage in front of an audience.

**Harmony**  The way different voices blend together.

**Lyrics**  The words of a song.

**Melody**  The tune of a piece of music or song.

**Orchestra**  A large group of performers playing various musical instruments together.

**Pitch**  A high musical note or sound is said to have a high pitch. A low musical note or sound is said to have a low pitch.

**Play**  A dramatic performance on stage.

**Range**  From the highest to the lowest.

**Sound wave**  A wave that transmits sound through the air.

**Symbol**  A shape used to represent something.

**Symphony**  A piece of instrumental music written for an orchestra.

**Tempo**  The speed at which music is played.

**Timbre**  The pitch and loudness of a sound.

**Tone**  The quality of a sound, or the kind of sound it is.

**Verses**  The main lyrics of a song.

**Vibrate; vibration**  Moving back and forth rapidly.

**Warm-up exercises**  Voice exercises done by singers to prevent their vocal cords being damaged when they perform.

# Index